Superfast TRAINS

by Mark Dubowski

Consultant: Courtney B. Wilson, Executive Director,
Baltimore & Ohio Railroad Museum

BEARPORT
PUBLISHING COMPANY, INC.

New York, New York

Credits

Cover, Courtesy of Transrapid International GmbH& Co. KG; Title Page, Courtesy of Transrapid International GmbH& Co. KG; 4, AP Wide World Photos; 5, Courtesy of Roger Stoutrenburgh/Brookhaven National Laboratory; 6, Courtesy of Transrapid International GmbH& Co. KG; 7, Courtesy of Dr. Kuhnl, Mrs. Quassowski, Nortrup Germany/ Transrapid International GmbH & Co. KG; 8(T), Courtesy of Trevithick Society and Cornwall and Isles of Scilly Press; 8(B), The Granger Collection, New York; 9, Courtesy of Phil Monkton/Trevithick Society and Cornwall and Isles of Scilly Press; 10-11, AP Wide World Photos; 12, Bettmann/Corbis; 13, AP Wide World Photos; 14, AP Wide World Photos; 15, age fotostock/SuperStock; 16, AP Wide World Photos; 17, AP Wide World Photos; 18, AP Wide World Photos; 19, Courtesy Transrapid International GmbH& Co. KG; 20, Koichi Kamoshida/Getty Images; 21, Koichi Kamoshida/Getty Images; 22-23, AP Wide World Photos; 24, AP Wide World Photos; 25, AP Wide World Photos; 26, AP Wide World Photos; 27, Courtesy Transrapid International GmbH& Co. KG.

Editorial development by Judy Nayer
Design & Production by Paula Jo Smith

Library of Congress Cataloging-in-Publication Data

Dubowski, Mark.

Superfast trains / by Mark Dubowski.

p. cm.—(Ultimate Speed)

Includes bibliographical references and index.

ISBN 1-59716-084-9 (library binding)—ISBN 1-59716-121-7 (pbk.)

1. High speed trains. I. Title. II. Series.

TF1450.D83 2006

385'.2—dc22

2005005526

For more information, write to Bearport Publishing Company, Inc., 101 Fifth Avenue, Suite 6R, New York, New York 10003. Printed in the United States of America.

1 2 3 4 5 6 7 8 9 10

CONTENTS

A New Kind of Train

The year was 1966. American **engineers** Gordon Danby and James Powell were hard at work.

On the highway near their lab, cars were stopped in traffic jams. At airports across the country, planes were stuck in bad weather. Everywhere, noise and smoke **pollution** was getting worse. Danby and Powell were looking for an answer to these problems.

Danby and Powell wanted to try to stop traffic jams like this one.

Their answer was a new kind of train. It would run without noise or smoke. It would run without an **engine**, and without wheels. The train would fly above the track. It would go almost as fast as an airplane soars across the sky!

Gordon Danby (left) and James Powell (right)

James Powell was stuck in traffic when he first came up with his idea for a new kind of train.

Maglev: Magnetic Levitation

The train Danby and Powell wanted to build was called a Maglev. *Maglev* is short for "magnetic levitation." The Maglev uses magnetic power to levitate, or lift, the train above the track.

Maglev trains have no wheels. Underneath the train are powerful **magnets**. Near these magnets, in the track, are thick electric wires.

The Maglev

Electricity in the wires creates a **magnetic field**. This force pushes against the magnets under the train. The lifting power of the magnetic field is strong enough to float the train above the track. The magnetic field then pushes the train at a superfast speed.

The "father of the Maglev" was German scientist Hermann Kemper. He first came up with the idea in 1922.

Maglev trains ride on air. They can go faster than trains that ride on rails because there is no **friction** to slow them down.

The First Trains

Trains have been around for about 200 years. The first train was powered by a **steam engine**. It was invented in England in 1804 by Richard Trevithick. The train was used to carry coal. It was strong, but it only went four miles per hour (6 kph). That's slower than a horse-drawn wagon.

Richard Trevithick

Trevithick's "Puffing Devil"

FIG. 93.—TREVITHICK'S LOCOMOTIVE, 1804.   THE FIRST TO RUN ON RAILS.

Trevithick called his **locomotive** the Puffing Devil because it puffed steam and "worked like the devil." Trevithick knew about steam engines from working in a mine. The mine used a steam engine to pump out water so men could work.

Today, museum visitors can see the Puffing Devil up close.

The Puffing Devil was not fast, but it was strong. Many horses would be needed to pull the same load.

As Fast as Steam Can Go

By the 1850s, steam locomotives were used all over the world. By 1900, steam trains were going 60 miles per hour (97 kph). Cars on today's highways go about that fast.

On May 11, 1936, a German train called the 4-6-4 Hudson left the city of Hamburg. It was headed for Berlin. Halfway there, the train hit a speed of 124 miles per hour (200 kph). Many people think it was the fastest steam locomotive ever. Others disagree. They say a British train called the Mallard was faster. It went 126 miles per hour (203 kph). However, the Mallard was going downhill. Also, it only went a short distance.

In the 1930s, speed records for steam trains were set that have never been beaten.

In 1935, Germany built the high-speed steam locomotives 4-6-4 Hudson 05 001 (shown here) and the 4-6-4 Hudson 05 002, which was clocked going over 120 miles per hour (193 kph).

Diesel-Electric Engines

The steam engine met its match in a new kind of train. In 1924, American engineers came up with an engine called the **diesel-electric**. It was a **hybrid** engine, with two kinds of power. It had a **piston** engine that was like a steam engine. The piston did not turn the wheels, though. It charged a battery. The battery ran an electric motor that then turned the wheels.

In 1892, German scientist Rudolph Diesel invented the engine named after him. Americans put his idea to work by adding an electric motor to make the diesel-electric train.

The piston engine did not have to work hard. The batteries did the work. The piston engine also didn't break down when the wheels turned at high speeds.

The Denver Zephyr was a diesel-electric train that carried passengers between Chicago and Denver.

Diesel-electric trains were faster than steam engine trains. In 1934, the Pioneer Zephyr went 1,015 miles (1,633 km) at an average speed of 77.6 miles per hour (124.8 kph).

Bullet Trains

In America, diesel-electric trains hauled **freight** at speeds of over 100 miles per hour (161 kph). Passengers who rode on trains, though, were switching to cars and trucks. So building faster trains to move people became less important.

In Japan, things were different. Roads were smaller. Gasoline prices were higher. Even people who had cars still rode trains.

Nearly one million people in Japan ride bullet trains every day.
Bullet trains were named for their shape and speed.

In 1964, while Danby and Powell were thinking about Maglev, Japan invented a new, superfast passenger train. They called it the "bullet train," or *Shinkansen*. These all-electric trains ran on wider tracks than Japan's old trains. They carried people long distances at over 125 miles per hour (201 kph).

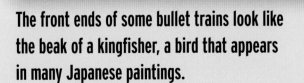

The front ends of some bullet trains look like the beak of a kingfisher, a bird that appears in many Japanese paintings.

Today, Japan's Nozomi bullet train is the fastest regular passenger train in the world. It has a top speed of 187 miles per hour (301 kph).

Train à Grande Vitesse

France faced the same transportation problems as Japan. So in 1981, the French opened a new high-speed passenger line called TGV. The letters TGV stand for *Train à Grande Vitesse*, the French words for "very fast train."

TGV trains average 186 miles per hour (299 kph). Other high-speed trains average 150 miles per hour (241 kph).

On May 18, 1990, the TGV Atlantique set the electric train speed record. It reached a speed of 322 miles per hour (518 kph).

Like Japan's bullet trains, the design of the TGV is **aerodynamic**. The engine and cars have a smooth, airplane-like shape. This feature helps the trains cut through the air faster than older trains.

TGV trains carry passengers through France into Belgium, Germany, Switzerland, Holland, England, and Italy.

The Shanghai Express

Danby and Powell watched the French and Japanese trains getting faster and faster. They were still sure that Maglev trains could beat anything on wheels.

So far, though, Maglev was still just an idea. No one had built one. In 1999, engineers in Germany were working on an idea that was a lot like Danby and Powell's.

Inside the Shanghai Maglev

In December of that year, China asked the German engineers to build their Maglev in Shanghai (SHANG-*hye*). Three years later, the test train was ready.

The world's first Maglev train raced from Shanghai's Pudong Airport to downtown Shanghai. It carried passengers at 267 miles per hour (430 kph)!

The 19-mile (31-km) trip from Pudong Airport to downtown Shanghai only takes eight minutes aboard the Maglev train.

Shanghai Maglev

The World's Fastest Train

China's test train was fast, but Danby and Powell knew Maglevs could be even faster. A new train in Japan proved they were right.

In 2003, a Maglev test train was built near Tokyo. The test train's track was only 11 miles (18 km) long. To break the world's speed record, the train had to **accelerate** quickly.

At over 300 miles per hour (483 kph), the speed of Maglev trains is coming closer to the speed of airplanes. Airplanes fly at speeds of 600 miles per hour (966 kph).

It did. On December 3, 2003, Japan's Maglev became the world's fastest train. It hit a top speed of 361 miles per hour (581 kph). For Maglev trains, though, the test was not over.

Japan's Maglev is the world's fastest train—so far.

The Next Maglev

China had the first Maglev. Japan had the fastest. Yet both of them were only **experimental** trains. They went short distances and did not carry many passengers.

German engineers said that the first real Maglev was coming to their country—soon. It would carry hundreds of passengers every day.

The engineers promised that thousands of people in the city of Munich (MYOO-nik) would be able to take a new Maglev train. It would take them from the train station to the airport in just ten minutes. It was a trip that normally took over an hour.

Germany's superfast InterCity Express (ICE) line will get even faster when it opens a Maglev to the public in Munich.

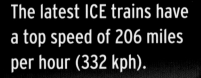

The latest ICE trains have a top speed of 206 miles per hour (332 kph).

Superfast Trains of Today

In some places, riders don't need Maglevs to get where they want to go quickly. In Europe, Eurostar trains travel between England, France, and Belgium. They connect these countries' capital cities—London, Paris, and Brussels. Each train can carry 700 passengers on one trip.

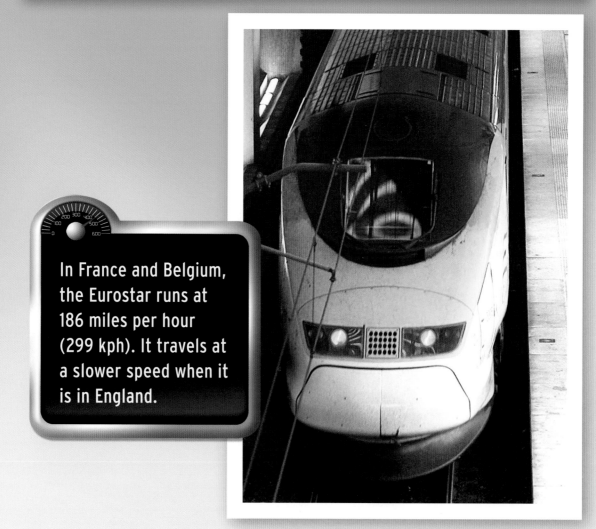

In France and Belgium, the Eurostar runs at 186 miles per hour (299 kph). It travels at a slower speed when it is in England.

In the United States, the Acela Express hits 150 miles per hour (241 kph) between Boston, New York, and Washington, D.C. *Acela* comes from the words "accelerate" and "excellence." The Acela cuts through the air with its smooth shape, just like Europe's high-speed trains.

On the Acela, riders travel at more than twice the speed of cars.

Superfast Trains of the Future

Engineers are working on Maglevs for America. Danby and Powell say special tunnels can be built that will make Maglev trains go *thousands* of miles per hour. They have plans to make the United States home of the world's first long-distance Maglev.

There are no Maglevs running in the United States yet. This model shows what these trains will look like.

Traffic jams, crowded airports, and pollution were problems in 1966. They are even bigger problems today. Maglev trains can be part of the solution.

Will it happen? Engineers like Danby and Powell say it will—and *fast*!

Plans are already underway to build a Maglev between Las Vegas and Southern California. The 270-mile (435-km) trip would take just 75 to 90 minutes!

- The first train was so slow that its inventor, Richard Trevithick, walked alongside it during its first trip.

- In 1869, the first U.S. transcontinental railway was completed. People could travel from coast to coast in six weeks by train. The same trip took six months by wagon.

- Today, a fleet of Eurostar trains called Le Shuttle travels underwater between England and France. It moves through a 31-mile (50-km) tunnel called the Channel Tunnel, or Chunnel. The trip takes about 20 minutes. Le Shuttle is the fastest underground train in the world.

TIMELINE   This timeline shows some important events in the history of superfast trains.

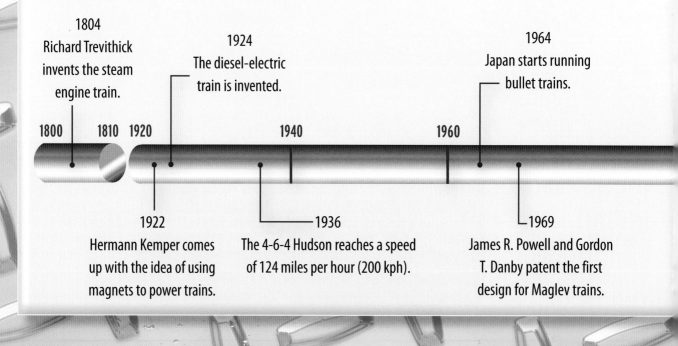

1804
Richard Trevithick invents the steam engine train.

1924
The diesel-electric train is invented.

1964
Japan starts running bullet trains.

| 1800 | 1810 | 1920 | | 1940 | | 1960 | |

1922
Hermann Kemper comes up with the idea of using magnets to power trains.

1936
The 4-6-4 Hudson reaches a speed of 124 miles per hour (200 kph).

1969
James R. Powell and Gordon T. Danby patent the first design for Maglev trains.

- In Japan, some bullet trains have two levels. They can carry up to 1,600 passengers.

- The fastest speed between two station stops is 164 miles per hour (264 kph) on Japan's Nozomi. This bullet train travels between Hiroshima and Kokkura.

- The longest train in the world is in Mauritania, Africa. It carries coal from the mountains to the sea. The train is 1.8 miles (2.9 km) long.

- The world's longest train ride is on the Trans-Siberian tracks across Russia. It takes seven days to cover the 5,777-mile (9,297-km) journey. The train crosses seven time zones.

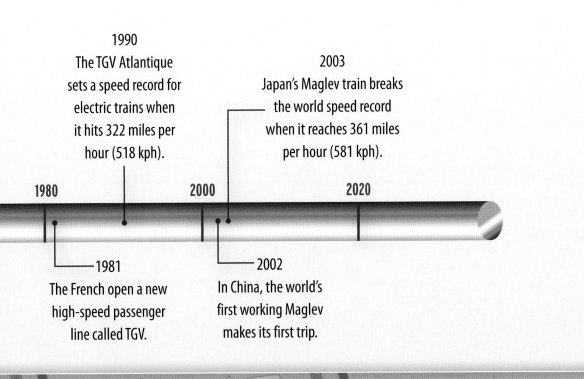

1990
The TGV Atlantique sets a speed record for electric trains when it hits 322 miles per hour (518 kph).

2003
Japan's Maglev train breaks the world speed record when it reaches 361 miles per hour (581 kph).

1980 2000 2020

1981
The French open a new high-speed passenger line called TGV.

2002
In China, the world's first working Maglev makes its first trip.

GLOSSARY

accelerate (ak-SEL-uh-*rate*) to speed up

aerodynamic (*air*-oh-dye-NAM-ik) designed to move quickly through the air

diesel-electric (DEE-zuhl-i-LEK-trik) an engine in which one part runs on diesel fuel and the other part on electricity

engine (EN-juhn) a machine that makes something move

engineers (en-juh-NIHRZ) people who are trained to design and build machines

experimental (ek-*sper*-uh-MEN-tuhl) related to a test, trial, or experiment to discover something unknown

freight (FRAYT) a load of goods or supplies

friction (FRIK-shuhn) the force created when one object rubs against another

hybrid (HYE-brid) in trains, an engine that has two parts that do the same thing and work together

locomotive (*loh*-kuh-MOH-tiv) an engine used to push or pull railroad cars; a train

magnetic field (mag-NET-ik FEELD) a force around a magnet that pushes or pulls other magnets or metal

magnets (MAG-nitz) pieces of metal that attract other metals

piston (PISS-tuhn) a small cylinder that moves back and forth within a larger cylinder

pollution (puh-LOO-shuhn) harmful materials that damage or dirty the air or water

steam engine (STEEM EN-juhn) an engine that heats water and uses the steam to move parts connected to the wheels

BIBLIOGRAPHY

www.american-maglev.com

www.factmonster.com/spot/trains1.html

www.japan-guide.com

www.railway-technology.com

READ MORE

Balkwill, Richard. *The Best Book of Trains.* Boston, MA: Kingfisher Books (1999).

Biello, David. *Bullet Trains: Inside and Out.* New York: PowerKids Press (2002).

Cefrey, Holly. *High Speed Trains.* New York: Children's Press (2001).

Coiley, John. *Eyewitness: Train.* New York: DK Publishing (2000).

Heap, Christine. *Big Book of Trains.* New York: DK Publishing (1998).

Maynard, Chris. *High-Speed Trains.* Minneapolis, MN: Lerner (2002).

LEARN MORE ONLINE

Visit these Web sites to learn more about trains:

www.msichicago.org/exhibit/zephyr

www.railwaymuseums.org

www.steamlocomotive.com

INDEX

ABOUT THE AUTHOR

Mark Dubowski is the author/illustrator of many books for young
readers. He took his first train ride with his grandparents when he
was seven years old. His favorite car was the "observation car."
It had stairs that led to seats in a glass room on top of the car.

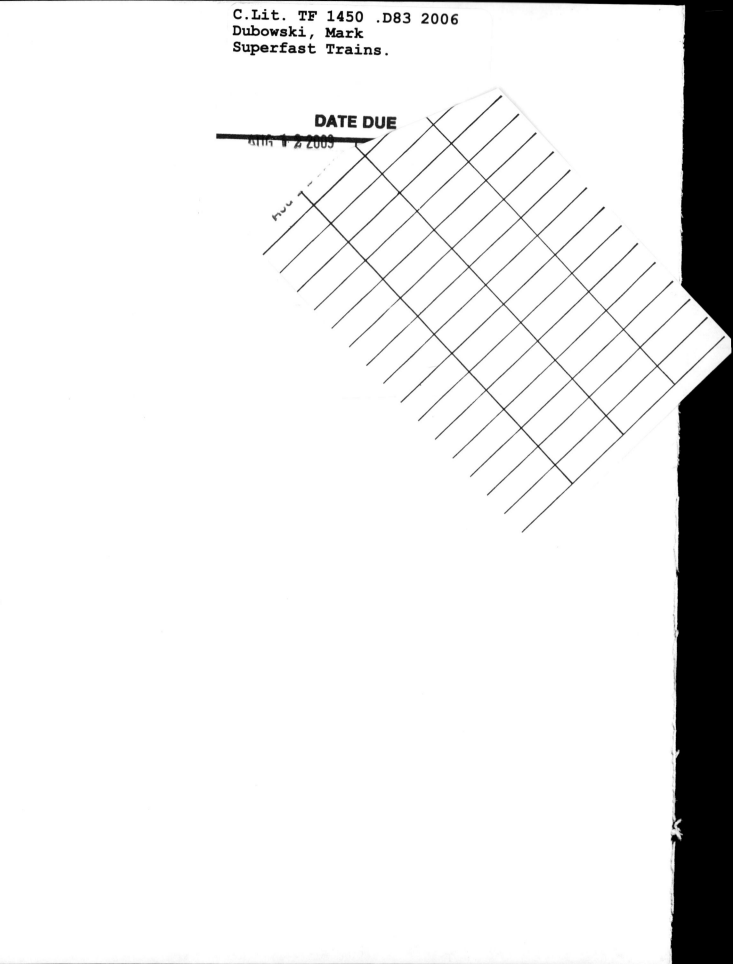